THE LOUISVILLE CARDINAL

UNBREAKABLE

LOUISVILLE'S INSPIRED 2013 CHAMPIONSHIP RUN

This book is available in quantity at special discounts for your group or organization.
For further information, contact:

Triumph Books LLC
814 North Franklin Street
Chicago, Illinois 60610
Phone: (312) 337-0747
www.triumphbooks.com

Printed in U.S.A.
ISBN: 978-1-60078-887-1

The Louisville Cardinal Inc. A nonprofit organization
Rae Hodge, Editor-in-Chief
Caitlyn Crenshaw, Managing Editor
Sammie Hill, Sports Editor
Noah Allison, Assistant Sports Editor
Austin Lassell, Photo Editor
Tricia Stern, Assistant Photo Editor
Lara Kinne, Copy Editor
Mickey Meece, Adviser/Book Editor
Contributors: Xavier Bleuel, Randy Whetsone Jr., Sam Draut and Jessica Knebel

Content packaged by Mojo Media, Inc.
Joe Funk: Editor
Jason Hinman: Creative Director

Front cover photo by Getty Images. Back cover photo by Austin Lassell/The Louisville Cardinal.

Austin Lassell/The Louisville Cardinal

CONTENTS

Introduction

'America's Team' Finds the Will to Win Louisville's Third National Championship

Pitino Melds a Mosaic of Talents, Skills and Backgrounds En Route to an 82-76 Win over Michigan

By Billy Reed

This is the enduring image of the 2013 NCAA men's basketball tournament: Louisville's Luke Hancock cradling the head of Kevin Ware in his arms and saying a prayer in the immediate aftermath of the most horrific injury in tournament history. It happened when Ware, flinging himself skyward while attempting to block a Duke player's shot, came down wrong on his right leg, causing the femur to snap and puncture Ware's skin. As soon as they saw it, Ware's teammates either recoiled in horror or fell to the floor, wailing and weeping.

Except, that is, for Hancock. As the arena went silent and even the CBS announcers were almost too shocked to talk, Hancock prayed in Ware's ear. A student manager draped a towel over the shattered leg to block it from view. Hearing Hancock, Ware reached deep into his soul and found a kind of grace that defies explanation. Even as he was going into shock, he urged his teammates to not worry about him, to carry on, to win the Midwest Regional championship and the ticket to hoops heaven—the

Final Four in Atlanta. And so they did. They wiped away their tears, pulled tightly together and blew out the mighty Blue Devils in the second half.

It went largely unnoticed that Ware is black and Hancock white. But for basketball fans old enough to have a sense of basketball's history and sociology, the Hancock-Ware tableau was symbolic. Throughout the history of the NCAA tournament, which celebrated its 75th anniversary this year, only a few champions have carried the name of a city instead of a state or, in the case of Georgetown University, a neighborhood. Forget UCLA and UNLV, which were the local branches of larger state university systems. The city schools that have won titles are City College of New York, San Francisco, Cincinnati, Loyola of Chicago, Syracuse, and, of course, Louisville.

In their home states, urban universities often get short shrift from the legislature and are considered to be second-class citizens by the public. In the late 1980s, for example, former Kentucky coach Eddie Sutton, ignoring the championship Cardinal

Rick Pitino, the only head coach to win national championships with two different NCAA teams, holds the trophy aloft. (Austin Lassell/The Louisville Cardinal)

teams coached by Peck Hickman and Denny Crum, dismissed U of L as "little brother." But what Sutton either didn't know—or chose to ignore—was that U of L and the other urban universities have made contributions to sports and society that were far more important than anything that happened on the floor.

Every time significant strides have been made in integration, urban universities have been in the forefront. San Francisco became the first integrated champion in 1955, Cincinnati the first to start three African-American players in 1962, and Loyola the first to start four blacks in 1963. When Hickman and assistant John Dromo recruited U of L's first African-American players in 1962, it made U of L the first predominantly white university in the state—the first south of the Mason-Dixon Line, according to some accounts—to integrate its program. This is a proud heritage of which Kevin Ware and Luke Hancock probably were unaware when they transferred from Tennessee and George Mason, respectively, to play for Rick Pitino, the native New Yorker who had won the 1996 national title at Kentucky and who also was the first coach to take three programs (Providence, UK and U of L) to the Final Four.

When they arrived at U of L, they found Pitino building a team not from one-and-done future NBA stars, but from players who had different backgrounds and skill levels. Sure, some had pro bodies and pro ambitions, such as forwards Wayne Blackshear and Chane Behanan. But there also was Stephen Van Treece, a 6-foot-9 player with marginal D-I skills. The team's core consisted of Gorgui Dieng, a stoic 6-foot-11 center from Africa who could speak five languages; Peyton Siva, a slight point guard from Seattle who was so nice it was

impossible to hold his trespasses—turnovers, if you will—against him; and a free spirit from Brooklyn whom Pitino called "Russdiculous" because of his penchant to put up shots that defied logic, not to mention the laws of gravity.

From the time Russ Smith arrived on campus, the mental tug-of-war between player and coach provided plenty of fascinating fodder for the talk shows and the fans. They truly seemed to have the sort of love-hate relationship that only a couple of New Yorkers could understand. Watching on TV back home in Queens, Smith's high school coach, the beloved Jack Curran of Archbishop Molloy, could only shake his head. "Timeouts, [Pitino] is always yelling at Russ," Curran told *Sports Illustrated* early this season. "And Russ puts his face right into Pitino's face. Like a soldier, he stands there. He's almost touching noses with him. He's very sober-looking while making believe that he's listening."

If Smith began to come around as the season unfolded, making better choices and become more team-oriented, his transformation became complete when he arrived in New York for the Big East Tournament in Madison Square Garden and learned that Curran had died unexpectedly of a heart attack. He dedicated his play to Curran and his teammates rallied around him, rolling to the tournament championship. In the title game against Syracuse, U of L trailed by 16 in the second half, only to have Smith, Silva and Ware ignite a second-half explosion in which they blew past the Orange and pulled away almost before Coach Jim Boeheim was able to work up one his famous scowls.

Still, though, the Cards didn't become America's Team until the Ware tragedy. Because it happened before the CBS cameras in one of the

Guard Kevin Ware, an inspiration for the team's Final Four run, cuts down the nets despite being limited on crutches. (Austin Lassell/The Louisville Cardinal)

tournament's most anticipated games, people around the globe became caught up in the sheer horror of the injury and the courageous way Pitino and the Cards responded. Suddenly the urban university from Louisville was feeling love it had never before received. Suddenly everyone became curious about the urban university located practically next door to Churchill Downs, home of the Kentucky Derby, and the changes that had been wrought since Tom Jurich became athletics director in 1998.

In the 15 years of the Jurich era, new arenas and stadiums have been built for every varsity sport, transforming the formerly drab campus into something vibrant and pleasing to the eyes of the millions who drove past every day on I-65. He also hired coaches who built teams that were nationally competitive in every sport. And most importantly, he insisted on full compliance with the NCAA rules and the provisions of Title IX. When plans were being made for the state-of-the-art KFC Yum! Center on the banks of the Ohio River, Jurich's main requirement was that the women's basketball team have a dressing room and practice court that was identical to the men.

The payoff has been stunning. On the very day the men's basketball team defeated Duke, while Kevin Ware was undergoing surgery on his shattered leg, the U of L women's team shocked defending NCAA champion Baylor in what was called the biggest upset in the history of the women's tournament. (Two days later, the women eliminated perennial power Tennessee to earn a berth in the Final Four.)

So, in a sense, what happened in Atlanta was anti-climactic. Ware already was entrenched as the poster child for the 75th NCAA tournament. His story had transcended the sport and made a U of L

championship seem almost ordained. The outpouring of love and support—not only for Ware, but also for the team—was overwhelming. It came in the form of letters and flowers, of tweets and texts, of sweet odes in major newspapers and the TV networks. It came from rich and poor, from young and old, from the famous and the faceless. It came from Oprah, Michelle Obama and little old ladies in Dubuque.

The national media suppressed its cynicism and talked—without fear of being accused of resorting to clichés—of how Pitino had turned his players from a collection of disparate parts into as much of a real "family" as a sports team can get. For Pitino, a model of humility throughout the tournament, it was redemption as both a coach and a person. Only a few years earlier, his career had been stained by a highly publicized personal scandal that shook the university and the city to its foundation. But time has healed Pitino's psyche as surely as it will Ware's leg. The morning after his surgery, Ware was on crutches and photographed admiring the Midwest Regional trophy that Pitino had brought to his hospital room.

While the basketball teams were feeling the nation's love, another team on campus was hard at work chronicling the events as they unfolded. It's always a tricky proposition to teach student journalists how to report fairly and accurately on their friends and classmates. When you've seen Luke Hancock or Kevin Ware in a pizza joint, maybe had a class with one of them, how can you possibly find perspective? But as the following pages prove, the staff of *The Cardinal*, the university's student newspaper, lived up to the motto the basketball players wore on the fronts of their warm-up shirts – *Rise to the Occasion!* ■

CBS announcer Jim Nantz speaks to Kevin Ware, who attended the Final Four in his hometown of Atlanta despite suffering a horrific leg injury the week before. (Austin Lassell/The Louisville Cardinal)

NCAA Championship Game

Game Date: April 8, 2013 · **Location:** Atlanta, Georgia
Score: Louisville 82, Michigan 76

Louisville Captures Third National Championship

Cards Cap Off Remarkable Season as 2013 NCAA National Champions

By Randy Whetstone Jr.

On a court filled with confetti, Gorgui Dieng was living an unfathomed dream: "To win the national championship, I never dreamed about this. I don't have any words for this. I just tried to do my job. I feel I did it tonight. Everyone was involved; that's what makes us a good basketball team."

Dieng's brother in the frontcourt, Chane Behanan, said: "I never knew it would feel like this. It feels like we are on the top of the world. Me and my brothers here, this is why we put in work all during the summer. Like coach told us, leave everything out on the court. Don't worry about making mistakes; take your chances—chances make champions."

In a championship game played in front of a record of 74,326 fans the University of Louisville men's basketball team won its first National Championship in 27 years, defeating the Michigan Wolverines 82-76.

The team has been characterized with unity, toughness and heart. After reaching the Final Four last season and falling short to Kentucky, Louisville bounced back with its eye on the prize. They started the season as preseason No. 2, and the team fought—ending the postseason No. 1. This is Louisville's first national championship since 1986. Outstanding Player of the Final Four Luke Hancock said, "It doesn't get better than this, it's unbelievable. It does not get better than this."

The first half was a Michael "Spike" Albrecht and Luke Hancock three-point shootout. Michigan was up by as many as 12 points. After the national player of the year Trey Burke went to the bench due to foul trouble, the freshman for the Wolverines stepped up. Albrecht hit four of the

Luke Hancock, the transfer from George Mason and Most Outstanding Player of the tournament, attempts a shot near the basket. (Austin Lassell/The Louisville Cardinal)

"I LOOK BACK ON IT AND SAY, THAT WAS REALLY, REALLY SPECIAL. I WAS GLAD TO BE PART OF THIS TEAM."

— Louisville Guard Kevin Ware

team's six three-point shots. He scored 17 of the team's 38 first-half points.

The Cards were in desperate need of a spurt on offense. Down 12 points in the first half, it was Hancock again for the Cardinals making his presence known. He scored 14 points in a 2:33 span. He hit four straight three-point shots, and Montrezl Harrell topped it off for the Cards after receiving the alley-oop slam from Peyton Siva to give Louisville its first lead of the game 37-36. In 13 minutes, Hancock went perfect from the field, 4-for-4 and scored a team high 16 points. Michigan led at the half 38-37.

In the second half, Trey Burke came out as the avenger after sitting most of the first half. He scored 17 points in the half and led his team the entire way. He showed his NBA potential when he hit a long-range bomb to cut into the Cards lead 54-52 with 12:07 to go. But the Cards kept the pressure on.

Siva had a huge second half, scoring 14 points, including an alley-oop slam assisted by Hancock which made the score 67-72 at the 6:27 mark. Behanan elevated to new heights in the second half. He took advantage on the offensive boards and ended the game with 15 points and 12 rebounds. Louisville turned the contest into a two-possession game, and Michigan could not overcome the deficit. Both teams had incredible offenses and the magnitude in which they played will go down as one the greatest college basketball championships ever to be played.

Hancock scored the most points by a bench player in a championship game in 49 years. He finished the game with 22 points going a perfect 5-for-5 from three-point

Backup center Zach Price holds up a sign, showing that Louisville, the No. 1 overall seed, earned the ultimate prize of the 2013 season. (Austin Lassell/The Louisville Cardinal)

land and was named Most Outstanding Player of the Final Four and was thrilled about playing in front of his father.

"I'm so excited for this team to be in this situation," Hancock said. "It's been a long road. There's no way to describe how I feel that my dad was here. It's hard to put into words. I'm so excited that he was here. It just means a lot. Just blessed to be in this situation. I'm just so happy for our team. I'm happy that multiple guys got to contribute on this great run. Everybody from Tim Henderson on. It's just great for our team. I'm so happy for these guys."

Wayne Blackshear loved every second of being champion. "This is a great feeling," he said. "You know when that buzzer sounded and we knew we had it sealed, and we knew we was the champion, it was the best feeling in my life."

Russ Smith spoke about Coach Pitino's halftime speech. "He said, you know we back in it. We down one, so we got a game now, let's go out there and finish the game. Let's go out and win, we got 20 minutes to be national champion."

The Cardinals were able to win the championship despite losing guard Kevin Ware to a gruesome leg injury during Louisville's Elite Eight win over Duke. "It is not about me," Ware said. "I am not that type of guy. Our team came out here and beat a great Michigan team. These are my brothers. They got the job done and I am so proud of them."

During the cutting of the nets, the rim was lowered for Ware to cut the last piece of the net. It was an emotional time in Card Nation. "It's been such a rollercoaster of emotions," Ware said. "I've been around when guys blow out their ACLs, but I've never seen such affection and spontaneous emotion. I look back on it and say, that was really, really special. I was glad to be part of this team."

Senior Peyton Siva has left his stamp in the Louisville Cardinal history books. "Well, I just got to thank God for blessing me with this opportunity," Siva said. "Winning this game, the whole game."

Center Gorgui Dieng, who had eight rebounds, six assists and three blocks during the 82-76 win versus Michigan, cuts down part of the net. (Austin Lassell/The Louisville Cardinal)

When asked about his legacy he shared, Siva responded: "My job was to continue to try to lead. That's always been my job as a point guard. Coach Pitino gave me an opportunity to run this team, and that's what I have always been trying to do. My legacy that I want to leave is to keep God first over everything, and put your teammates above all. You just got to continue to go out there and play for your team and play for the name on the front not on the back."

In his 28th collegiate season coaching and 12th with Louisville, Coach Rick Pitino is the first coach to take three different schools to Final Fours, and he became the first coach in college basketball to win two national championships at two different schools—Kentucky in 1996 and Louisville in 2013. Earlier on Monday, it was announced that Pitino will be part of the 2013 class of the Naismith Basketball Hall of Fame.

Pitino improved his NCAA Tournament record to 48-16. As the higher seed, his teams are 39-6. "You know, a lot of times when you get to the Final Four, you get to the championship, the game's not always great, not always pretty," Pitino said. "This was a great college basketball game. It's just, for us, been an incredible run with just the most wonderful young men I had the pleasure to be around. So proud of them."

Louisville finished the season with a 35-5 record and won its last 16 games, not losing in exactly two months. Since the five-overtime thriller at Notre Dame Feb. 9, the Cardinals played at another level. Their 35 wins are the most in the school's legacy. They are one of eight schools with three or more national championships, in company with UCLA, Kentucky, Indiana, North Carolina, Connecticut, Duke and Kansas. In the final season of the Big East, Louisville earned a share of the regular season championship, made a dramatic comeback versus Syracuse to win the Big East tournament and seized the ultimate reign as the 2013 NCAA National Champions. ■

The Louisville players celebrate the school's third national championship and first since 1986. (Austin Lassell/The Louisville Cardinal)

LUKE HANCOCK BRINGS THE THREES

By Sammie Hill

The first half of the National Championship appeared bleak for Louisville until Luke Hancock stepped in and gave an inspired performance. The Virginia native helped Louisville secure an 82-76 victory over Michigan and was named the Final Four's Most Outstanding Player.

Hancock remained solid on Monday night when the rest of the team seemed a step behind the Wolverines. Determined to keep Louisville from falling behind in the first half, Hancock scored 14 points in two and a half minutes. Sinking three-pointer after three-pointer, Hancock kept the Cardinals in the game and provided the team—and the Louisville crowd—with much needed momentum.

"We needed a rally, and we've been doing it for a couple of games straight, being down," Hancock said. "We just had to wait and make our run."

Driven by the personal motto to "play hard and have fun," the junior forward has made an impact since arriving at Louisville last year. The 6-foot-6, 200 pound player transferred to U of L from George Mason University last season. Hancock's transfer status forced him to sit out the 2011-12 season. Nevertheless, Hancock earned the title of co-captain this year due to his leadership abilities on and off the court. He clearly displayed this leadership Monday night.

"I just thought we needed something," Hancock said. "I tried to do whatever I could to help the team. I usually take a back seat to Russ and Peyton, which I'm fine with since they are such great players. I just hit a few shots."

Although Hancock recognized the significance of Monday's game, he tried to maintain a steady mindset.

"In the game, you just try to treat it like any other game," Hancock said. "Just try to go out there and play. If you're open, shoot it. If you're not, drive it and pass it to another guy."

With 22 points, Hancock made all five of these three-point attempts Monday night and led the Cardinals to their first NCAA victory since 1986. With leading scorer Russ Smith struggling, Hancock stepped up to keep Louisville in the game.

"As soon as we started playing Luke Hancock more, our halfcourt offense evolved into something that was very special. Luke is a play maker along with Peyton," said Coach Rick Pitino.

Luke Hancock nailed all five of his three-point attempts during the 82-76 championship victory. (Austin Lassell/The Louisville Cardinal)

"THESE ARE MY BROTHERS, THEY GOT THE JOB DONE. I'M SO PROUD OF THEM, SO PROUD OF THEM."

— Louisville Guard Kevin Ware

"Coach Pitino made this feel like home. I'm so excited for our team to be in this situation and finally be here," said Hancock.

Sunday Pitino added, "His father getting to that game, being there, was awesome."

"There's no way to describe how it feels that my dad was here," said Hancock.

As senior guard Peyton Siva and sophomore forward Chane Behanan began to contribute, Louisville gained the advantage and clung to victory as Hancock's three-pointer with 3:27 left put Louisville up double digits for the first time all game. The Cardinals were able to hold onto victory.

"It doesn't get any better than this," Hancock said after the game.

Injured guard Kevin Ware mirrored Hancock's excitement.

"These are my brothers," Ware said. "They got the job done. I'm so proud of them, so proud of them." ∎

Junior Luke Hancock, the wily co-captain who has battled injuries all year, looks to take advantage of Michigan freshman Nik Stauskas. (Austin Lassell/ The Louisville Cardinal)

NCAA Tournament Semifinal

Game Date: April 6, 2013 · **Location:** Atlanta, Georgia
Score: Louisville 72, Wichita State 68

Cardinals Oust Scrappy Shockers with Late Rally

Louisville Advances to Meet Michigan for NCAA Title

By Randy Whetstone Jr.

Louisville advanced to the NCAA Championship Game to compete for its third national championship, after coming from behind to beat the feisty Wichita State Shockers, 72-68.

The Cards have won 15 in a row and compiled a 34-5 record—the most wins in team history. Michigan defeated Louisville's Big East foe Syracuse, 61-56, in the other semifinal contest to set up the title game—Louisville's first since winning it all in 1986.

After the tense win, forward Chane Behanan said: "Having not been in a national championship [since] I don't know when, before I was born, and having the most wins in Louisville history, that's big, too. I'm glad to be a part of this tradition; it's just an honor and a blessing."

Luke Hancock came off the bench in the first half but started the second half and led a late rally for the tournament's No. 1 overall seed, scoring 14 of his 20 points in the second half. Hancock hit a clutch three-point shot, which gave Louisville a five-point lead, 65-60, with 2:06 remaining in the ballgame.

That provided enough cushion for the Cards as they nursed a small lead, and a two-possession game. Free throws by Russ Smith and Hancock sealed the win for Louisville 72-68 placing them in position to win a national championship.

As a whole, Louisville didn't play with the dominant demeanor everyone has been accustomed to. Many starters struggled and Coach Rick Pitino gave credit to Wichita State.

"Four of our starters had their worst night of the season," Pitino said. "We had to win this game with our second unit of Stephen Van Treese, a walk-on; Tim Henderson; one of the best six men in all of basketball, Luke Hancock;

Luke Hancock drives to the basket. Hancock came off the bench to score 20 points against Wichita State. (Austin Lassell/The Louisville Cardinal)

Luke Hancock battles Wichita State's Ron Baker for position. In 31 minutes, Hancock contributed two steals, two assists, and four rebounds in addition to 20 points. (Austin Lassell/The Louisville Cardinal)

"LUKE [HANCOCK] IS AN EXCELLENT PLAYER AND AN EXCELLENT PERSON. HE REALLY SHOWED HIS LEADERSHIP OUT THERE TONIGHT."

— Louisville Guard Peyton Siva

and Montrezl Harrell. There's a reason our starters played poorly: it's because Wichita State is that good. So we're really happy to play in the final game."

Louisville fans tried to rally the team and especially to pull for the injured Kevin Ware, holding "Win for Ware" signs. Ware was present with his teammates physically on the sideline, and present with the team spiritually on the court. In his physical absence on the court, Hancock picked up the slack. Senior guard Peyton Siva had a poor shooting night, going 1-for-9 from the field, 0-for-5 from three point land, was encouraged by the efforts of his teammate.

"Luke is an excellent player and an excellent person," Siva said of the co-captain. "He really showed his leadership out there tonight. He showed his leadership when Kevin got injured. He's just an all-around great player and person. Tonight, he showed the world what he is capable of doing."

The Cardinals found themselves in unfamiliar territory when they were down 12 in the second half. Russ Smith led the team with 21 points and explained his emotions when his team was so far behind.

"I feel like when it went to 12, I looked at it and the time kept going down and we kept fouling," Smith said. "I was actually waiting for our run, and it happened; Luke exploded, then Chane exploded. It kept going and going, and obviously I knew it wasn't my night, but I was so happy to see everyone else contributing, it was so special."

One unlikely contributor was walk-on guard Tim Henderson. Henderson gave oxygen for Louisville when

Wayne Blackshear reaches in for the ball against the Shockers. (Austin Lassell/The Louisville Cardinal)

"WE JUST PLAYED SUPER HARD. NOBODY WANTED TO GO HOME. WICHITA STATE DID A GREAT JOB OF HANGING WITH US, STICKING WITH THEIR GAME."

— Louisville Guard Russ Smith

everyone in red was gasping for air. Behanan, who finished with 10 points and nine rebounds, commended his teammate for hitting two three-pointers to cut the lead to six.

"He does that in practice all the time, and I'm just happy it converted when it counted, Behanan said. "He gave us two big three's down in the clutch. He contributed with Luke, myself, and Russ and I'm just happy we pulled it out."

Siva, in assessing his performance with seven points, said, "It was just one of those nights." After exalting his teammates, Siva said, "I just wanted to win. That's all that mattered to me, whether my shot was falling or not, as long as we won I was fine with how everything panned out."

Smith was pleased with the effort as Louisville dug in deep to rally to victory. "We just played super hard," Smith said. "Nobody wanted to go home. Wichita State did a great job of hanging with us, sticking with their game. We just fought really hard."

Coach Pitino will be coaching for his second National Championship. His win percentage in tournament play is 74 percent, ranking him fifth among active coaches, and 13th all-time. He has led Louisville to three final fours, with 2013 marking his first attempt at finishing the season on top. Louisville will have one day to prepare for the grand finale versus the Michigan Wolverines. The Wolverines and Cardinals boast the two best backcourts in the nation; the Wolverines' effort is led by Trey Burke, who was recently named national player of the year. ∎

Luke Hancock (right) celebrates with Tim Henderson after Henderson hit one of his two three-pointers. The two shots by Henderson, a walk-on, cut Wichita State's lead to six points with 12:18 remaining in the second half. (Austin Lassell/The Louisville Cardinal)

Louisville Women's Squad Joins Men in Final Four

Part of Magical Basketball Season, Louisville Women Knock Out Baylor, Tennessee

By Xavier Bleuel

Within 48 hours of knocking off Brittney Griner and the No. 1 overall seed Baylor Bears, the Louisville Cardinals shocked the world again with an upset over second-seeded and perennial power Tennessee 86-78 on Tuesday night in Oklahoma City.

The Schimmel sisters, Shoni and Jude, combined for 39 points, including six crucial threes. Shoni was named the regional MVP after her 24-point performance against the Vols.

Louisville is the 10th school to have both its men's and women's teams reach the Final Four in the same season. UConn, which has three teams on the list, most recently accomplished the feat back in 2011. Also, with the victory, for the first time ever, the Big East conference will have three members in the women's Final Four.

After finishing third in the Big East and losing to Notre Dame by 24 in the conference tournament semifinals, a win was not expected of the Cards. Most experts had them losing in the second round in Purdue, the ones who did not only had them advancing one more round to then fall to the favorite Baylor Bears.

"Nobody wanted us to be here," an ecstatic Shoni Schimmel said after the game. "Nobody wanted us to beat Baylor, and no one wanted us to beat Tennessee, but guess what? We did both."

Now the Cardinals, who join Southwest Missouri State's 2001 team as the only two fifth-seeded clubs to reach the Final Four, face the California Golden Bears in New Orleans with the right to play either Connecticut or Notre Dame.

The Cardinals didn't let their last loss to the Fighting Irish deter them from entering the tournament with some confidence.

"Yes, we lost to Notre Dame. But who doesn't, right?" Shoni Schimmel said of the Irish, whose only defeat this season was to Baylor in December. "We knew it was NCAA tournament time. Time to dance. That was when we started to peak."

And peak they did. After running over Middle

Louisville center Sheronne Vails battles for the ball during the Cardinals' second-round NCAA Tournament win over Purdue. (Austin Lassell/The Louisville Cardinal)

"NOBODY WANTED US TO BEAT BAYLOR, AND NO ONE WANTED US TO BEAT TENNESSEE, BUT GUESS WHAT? WE DID BOTH."

— Louisville Guard Shoni Schimmel

Tennessee State and Purdue at home, the Cardinals met Baylor and decided they wanted to be physical, drawing the ire from former Baylor quarterback Robert Griffin III in the process, claiming the fifth-seeded Cardinals (28-8), were "too physical" in their play against Griner, the unanimous All-America selection.

Whether it was too physical or not, the Cardinals got the job done, pulling off what some have called the biggest upset in women's college basketball history.

Then they had to regroup and face the second-seeded Lady Volunteers, who had not been to the Final Four since 2008. They came out firing on all cylinders, like they did against Baylor, jumping out to a 49-29 lead just a minute in to the second half.

When Tennessee made a valiant effort to cut the lead to three at 68-65 with over four minutes remaining, the Cardinals did not succumb to the pressure. Then the Cards went on a 7-0 run with Jude Schimmel hitting a three and her sister Shoni converting on two layups. The Vols just could not get close enough after Monique Reid iced the game with free throws at the end.

"We're the ugly ducklings of the tournament," Coach Jeff Walz said afterward. "But hey, we like it that way." ▪

Junior guard Antonita Slaughter (right) shares a moment with sophomore backcourt-mate Jude Schimmel. A Louisville native, Slaughter scored 21 points in Louisville's upset of top-ranked Baylor in the Sweet 16. (Austin Lassell/The Louisville Cardinal)

In 2013, Louisville became the 10th school to have both its men's and women's basketball teams reach the Final Four in the same season. Louisville joined Connecticut and Notre Dame in New Orleans to give the Big East three quarters of the Women's Final Four. (Austin Lassell/The Louisville Cardinal)

3
GUARD

PEYTON SIVA

Senior Point Guard Runs the Cardinals' Show

By Noah Allison • November 13, 2012

Every team needs a leader, a figurehead that the players can turn to and the coaches can trust in. A player who has been there, done that, but sure enough isn't finished yet. The 2012-2013 Louisville Cardinals have that, and it comes in the form of senior team captain Peyton Siva.

Siva leads the Cardinals storming back off a Final Four appearance last season. A deep and talented team filled with plenty of youth, as the only starting senior, and at point guard, it was only natural for Siva to take responsibility of trying to get the Cards back.

"I just want us to go hard and get back to where we were last year, only make it one game further," Siva said.

Siva was named preseason first team All-American and was named Big East preseason Player of the Year. He can get the job done on all areas of the court: getting steals, scoring points and, in true point guard fashion, spreading out assists. Last season, his 211 assists were second highest ever for a single U of L season. His 449 career assists, before the start of the 2012-13 season, rank eighth all time at U of L.

The Seattle native didn't start playing basketball until his sixth grade year, and back then the now six-foot point guard played center. His years of growth and maturity culminate here in his senior year at U of L. Siva has a rare, selfless talent that he uses to make the whole team thrive on the floor together. He is constantly working to improve the offense and make it more fluid.

"We have a lot of room for improvement, I think we have to do a lot better at communicating and talking more," Siva said.

The vocal player on the court, Siva has become used to talking from the swarm of reporters enclosing him in his locker after every news conference. The life of a super-talented team captain brings a lot of attention to the senior in college.

"I'm team captain, so it means I have to answer a lot questions," Siva said. "I take everything for my team. They trust me to be captain so they trust me to speak."

Siva was even featured on the cover of *Sports Illustrated*'s annual college basketball preview issue.

Cardinals point guard Peyton Siva maneuvers under the basket during Louisville's Feb. 14 win over St. John's. During his final season at Louisville, the senior was named Big East Tournament MVP for the second straight year in 2013 and broke the school's career steals record. (Austin Lassell/The Louisville Cardinal)

The matured player has the role of both leading his team and bringing them along to grow as both teammates and human beings.

"Don't get frustrated. Everything is going to happen for a reason. There are going to be times when you don't get the pass you wanted or things are just going wrong, but you have to keep your confidence up, and keep playing hard," Siva said.

Each player on the team is a necessity, and each plays his own special part. But Siva brings a special un-teachable quality to the team. All he can do is lead by example and let his class and composure wear off on the rest of the team.

Despite all the focus on No. 2 Louisville and the attention that Siva receives on a daily basis, he still manages to keep his senior year and the basketball season in perspective.

"I don't feel like we have any pressure at all. What do we have to live up to? We are just taking it one game at a time and continuing to play," Siva said. ∎

"DON'T GET FRUSTRATED. EVERYTHING IS GOING TO HAPPEN FOR A REASON. THERE ARE GOING TO BE TIMES WHEN YOU DON'T GET THE PASS YOU WANTED OR THINGS ARE JUST GOING WRONG, BUT YOU HAVE TO KEEP YOUR CONFIDENCE UP, AND KEEP PLAYING HARD."
— Louisville Guard Peyton Siva

As a senior, Peyton Siva became Louisville's 64th career 1,000 point scorer. (Austin Lassell/The Louisville Cardinal)

Star Point Guard Sets the Bar for Student Athletes

By Randy Whetstone Jr.

The point guard position is arguably the most important role on the basketball court. It serves as the core, nucleus and foundation of the offense. Every coach loves to have a floor general that operates as the coach on the court. U of L men's basketball Coach Rick Pitino has found this in senior point guard Peyton Siva.

Siva has evolved tremendously in his collegiate career. His growth in leadership has been immeasurable for Louisville men's basketball. The transcendence in his basketball skill has come from dedication and commitment. He has followed the commission of his role as point guard over the course of four years, and those leadership abilities have filtered into his classroom performance. Peyton Siva was named to the 2012-13 Capital One Academic All-America Division I Men's Basketball Team.

Siva majors in sociology and is the second selection ever from the University of Louisville men's basketball program to the Academic All-America team. Siva made the second team for the Academic All-America team, while Aaron Craft of Ohio State, Mason Plumlee of Duke, Kelly Olynyk of Gonzaga and Cody Zeller of Indiana were members of the first team.

This achievement by Siva can be used as a model for college athletes around the country. Every coach dreams of having a player of great talent as well as a player dedicated to great academic achievement. This academic success is another component Siva can add to his resume. Those who know him agree his leadership and passion add to his character. He embraces the opportunities to be the best basketball player and student he can be.

The Cardinals' point guard averages 5.8 assists a game — the third highest in the Big East. His 2.1 steals per game is also third in the conference. Earlier in the 2012-13 season, he became the Cardinals' 64th player to make the 1,000-point scoring club. His 607 career assists ranks second all-time at U of L, and all he needs is 12 steals to pass Darrell Griffith for the school record. Siva is also one of 12 finalists for the 2013 Bob Cousy Collegiate Point Guard of the Year award, awarded to the nation's top point guard. Peyton Siva added an additional milestone Feb. 23rd during the Seton Hall game with his 100th career start.

In this era of Division 1 basketball, the fad has been to go to school for one year and then declare for the NBA Draft. The issue that accompanies this trend has been the lack of zeal for students to take their studies seriously. Siva has worked to offset those statistics by being a McDonald's All-American and taking the initiative to excel in all academic areas.

During his time at the University of Louisville, Siva has earned a 3.37 cumulative grade point average. This academic recognition, along with his dominance on the court, demonstrates Siva's combination of mental and physical framework, which speaks volumes to underclassmen and incoming recruits. The notion would be to set a trend to engender academic priority for student-athletes in the future. ■

Peyton Siva excels in the classroom as well as on the hardcourt. Siva was awarded the Frances Pomeroy Naismith Award in 2013 based on his leadership, character, loyalty, all-around basketball ability and excellence in the classroom. (Austin Lassell/The Louisville Cardinal)

Regular Season

Game Date: December 29, 2012 · **Location:** Louisville, Kentucky
Score: Louisville 80, Kentucky 77

Battle of the Bluegrass

Louisville Outlasts Kentucky, Delighting Fans

By Sammie Hill

Making the list as one of Russ Smith's top five favorite victories of his career, the University of Louisville defeated the defending national champions, the University of Kentucky, 80-77, on Dec. 29. Smith scored 21 points and earned seven rebounds to help secure the win for the Cardinals.

"Overall, I'm delighted," Coach Rick Pitino said. "I thought we were brilliant in the first half on offense and defense. I think this team is very deep, and I'm not afraid to use people. Quite frankly, I don't think we are anywhere near our potential."

"Hats off to them," Kentucky Coach John Calipari said. "What a good team they are. They play hard, they play aggressive, they play rough, they have size, and their guard play is outstanding."

The match between Louisville and Kentucky, known as the "Battle of the Bluegrass," is renowned as one of the most intense in-state rivalries in the country. Though, the Cardinals revealed that the rivalry seems to ignite more fervor in the fans than in the players.

"This is a real important game for the fans," Pitino explained. "For us, we want to beat Kentucky, but not as much as the fans want to."

"For our fans, this is like a national championship game," senior guard Peyton Siva, continued. "This feels good for them."

"We're actually more happy for our fans than for ourselves," admitted Smith.

Entering the game with visible intensity, Louisville outscored Kentucky in the first half 36-28. However, Kentucky responded by outscoring Louisville in the second half 49-44. Louisville struggled with foul trouble throughout the game, but Kentucky's free throw shooting fell short; the Wildcats shot 11 of 23, or 48 percent.

"This is a great win for us because we had to battle a lot of bad foul trouble," Pitino said. "We survived with good play from Chane and Russ, but the defense and offense in the first half were

Russ Smith scored 21 points and grabbed seven rebounds as Louisville defeated cross-state rival Kentucky, 80-77. (Austin Lassell/The Louisville Cardinal)

"I THOUGHT WE WERE BRILLIANT IN THE FIRST HALF ON OFFENSE AND DEFENSE. I THINK THIS TEAM IS VERY DEEP AND I'M NOT AFRAID TO USE PEOPLE. QUITE FRANKLY, I DON'T THINK WE ARE ANYWHERE NEAR OUR POTENTIAL."

— Louisville Coach Rick Pitino

both spectacular. We just lost our defensive presence in the second half because we were worried about foul trouble."

Pitino also credited several other players as playing a crucial role in Saturday's win.

"Luke, Wayne, Kevin are all improving," Pitino explained. "Now, you have Chane who has elevated his game up there where Peyton and Russ are at, and now Gorgui is back."

Gorgui Dieng, the 6-foot-11 junior center, returned Saturday after sitting out seven games due to a broken left wrist. Dieng had six points, seven rebounds and two blocks.

"Gorgui is a hell of a basketball player," Pitino said. "He is a very smart young man. He knows how to make the right plays at the right time."

Sophomore forward Chane Behanan, who had 20 points, seven rebounds and three steals in Saturday's game, elaborated on the importance of this victory not only for the team but also for the entire city of Louisville.

"It just feels good to win," Behanan acknowledged, "not just for me but the city, too."

Smith agreed with Behanan's assessment of the significance of the Cardinals' triumph.

"It's a great win for the city," he said.

The University of Louisville men's basketball team will seek to learn from Saturday's game, incorporating the lessons and carrying the momentum into the rest of the season. ∎

Peyton Siva scored 19 points in 31 minutes as Louisville topped defending national champion Kentucky.
(Austin Lassell/The Louisville Cardinal)

Peyton Siva guards Kentucky freshman Archie Goodwin. Goodwin led the Wildcats with 22 points. (Austin Lassell/The Louisville Cardinal)

10
CENTER

GORGUI DIENG

Louisville's Renaissance Man Holds Center Court

By Rae Hodge

Take a 6-foot-11 polyglot and make him your center. Then add 50 pounds of muscle over the course of two years. From there, give him a 3.2 shot blocks per game and a 53 percent field goal average.

Put all that together and what have you got? A fortress of Louisville Cardinal defense who uses his 7-foot-4 wingspan to swat your shot, and who can call himself a champion in five different languages.

That's Gorgui Dieng.

"I came as a boy to this university, and I can tell you I'm a man right now," Dieng said. "I learned a lot of things." Including life lessons from Coach Rick Pitino. "Coach P, he didn't just teach me about basketball; he teaches me about life."

Dieng's journey from Kebemer, Senegal to Louisville, hasn't been easy for him, but since exploding onto U of L courts as a freshman, his upward momentum has been unceasing. He attributes much of that to the people he now calls family.

"When I was in high school, you know, I feel bad because I left family, friends, everybody home," Dieng confided to Card TV. "But now I feel like my teammates are my family. Coach P and everybody loves me, you know. I feel safe."

If safety really comes in numbers, then the Cardinals can feel as safe as Dieng; his numbers are record-breaking.

By his sophomore year, Dieng had blocked shots in 61 of his 69 career games, with multiple swats in 46 games. In 21 career games, he blocked at least four shots, 16 of those on the season. In back-to-back games he's shut down the opposition with at least five blocked shots on four occasions. That kind of smack down had never before been seen in U of L history.

Coach Pitino knows exactly where to put that kind of talent.

"When I showed my family and friends where I play," said Dieng, "they just couldn't believe it. I showed them everything but it's just so nice. I was

Gorgui Dieng shoots over St. John's Sir'Dominic Pointer. Louisville's big man had 17 rebounds against the Red Storm. (Austin Lassell/The Louisville Cardinal)

shocked the first time I got to the Yum! Center. When I get there with 20,000 people, everybody yelling your name, everybody, you know, gets hyped."

That kind of rapid progress tends to pressure-cook most athletes, but not Dieng. The lovable giant with academic aptitude has proved time and again that he is not most people.

"I've been here about three years, and I'm still the same Gorgui (pronounced GOR-gee): you're always going to see me smiling, going to school, playing basketball and doing fun stuff with my friends," Dieng said. "I came to Louisville and I know it's the right place to be—nice city, good people and I stay here. I like it here. I feel like I'm home."

It's been said that a man's home is his castle. If that's still the case, then woe unto the team that lays siege against U of L; Dieng's defense will surely be there to knock back the offensive tide. ■

"I CAME TO LOUISVILLE AND I KNOW IT'S THE RIGHT PLACE TO BE—NICE CITY, GOOD PEOPLE AND I STAY HERE. I LIKE IT HERE. I FEEL LIKE I'M HOME."

— Louisville Center Gorgui Dieng

Gorgui Dieng, who hails from Kebemer, Senegal, has become a reliable scorer and a dominating interior defender. (Austin Lassell/The Louisville Cardinal)

Regular Season

Game Date: January 28, 2013 · **Location:** Louisville, Kentucky
Score: Louisville 64, Pittsburgh 61

Bench Players Key a 64-61 Win Over Pitt

Cards End Panthers' Four-Game Win Streak

By Xavier Bleuel

Louisville crossed over to the win column as they defeated the Pittsburgh Panthers 64-61 on Monday night, ending Pittsburgh's four-game winning streak. Russ Smith exploded out of the gate, scoring eight of the team's first 10 points in usual "russdiculous" fashion, taking what seems like the whole team on fast breaks and scoring or drawing a foul. He finished as the game's leading scorer with 20 points on 7-of-15 shooting from the floor with five rebounds.

The Cardinals were playing without a starter and two key role players as Wayne Blackshear and Stephan Van Treese were out with injuries while Kevin Ware was suspended. Those losses loomed large, but several other players gained the opportunity to showcase their talent on the court. Michael Baffour, or "Dark Slime" as head coach Rick Pitino calls him, came in to play a few minutes, and Tim Henderson, a walk-on, came off the bench to play a solid 14 minutes.

After the game, Henderson shared his thoughts on taking over for Luke Hancock after the junior forward faced foul trouble.

"I've never played that spot in my life," Henderson revealed, "so having to come out and play against Pitt was just something else. But the coaches did a great job of telling me where to go and where to be. I just thought to myself, 'Play as hard as you can.'"

Henderson hit a 3-pointer in the first half, helping to build Louisville's lead.

"I was nervous out there," Henderson

Peyton Siva (left) and Gorgui Dieng defend Pitt's Trey Ziegler. Louisville's win snapped the Cardinals' three-game losing streak. (Austin Lassell/The Louisville Cardinal)

"SIVA JUST DID A GREAT JOB OF RUNNING HIS TEAM. HE WAS IN CONTROL THE WHOLE GAME. HE RAN HIS TEAM TO PERFECTION."

— Pitt Guard Tray Woodall

admitted, "but once I got going more and more, the more comfortable I got. My mindset was just to play hard."

Gorgui Dieng mirrored Henderson's positive outlook.

"This is a good win for us because Pitt is a good team," Dieng said. "I think this win will help us out a lot, and move our confidence up a little bit too. We take each game as very important. We are playing for a seed so we just bring it every night."

Dieng finished the game with 14 points, five blocks and four assists.

"We played a really good game tonight, made our free throws," Pitino said. "We did a lot of good things. Gorgui played a terrific game. I thought all the guys looked for each other, did a lot of good things."

The Cardinal front-court came to play as Behanan, Dieng and Harrell combined for 34 points and 22 rebounds. Pittsburgh did find a way to rally back however, erasing an 11-point deficit as they cut the lead to a basket at 60-58. Dieng and Smith sealed the game with four free throws at the end.

Despite scoring only two points, senior guard Peyton Siva dished out 10 assists. This marks the fifth game in which Siva has reached double digits in that category.

"I thought he was a major key in the game," Pitino said of Siva. "They couldn't turn us over because of that young man. He was a floor leader the whole way."

"Siva just did a great job of running his team," Panthers guard Tray Woodall added. "He was in control the whole game. He ran his team to perfection." ■

Peyton Siva dominated the game despite scoring only two points, dishing out 10 assists and collecting two steals while playing all 40 minutes. (Austin Lassell/The Louisville Cardinal)

11
FORWARD

LUKE HANCOCK

The Transfer Who Holds the Key

By Sam Draut • November 11, 2012

The No. 2 University of Louisville men's basketball team came into the 2012-13 season with high expectations based in large part on the players returning from the Final Four run a year ago. Returning starters Peyton Siva, Gorgui Dieng and Chane Behanan have received preseason accolades, but may not be the most critical part of the team.

Enter Luke Hancock, a 6-foot-6 junior who sat out the 2011-12 season after transferring from George Mason University. Hancock provides versatility to the U of L lineup; he starts at small forward, but can also play point guard.

Hancock began his career at George Mason, earning all-rookie team honors in the Colonial Athletic Association his freshman year, then averaging 10.9 points, 4.6 rebounds and 4.3 assists per game in his sophomore campaign.

Hancock sat out last season after transferring but was able to practice with the team. In U of L head coach Rick Pitino's final news conference of the spring, he announced Hancock and Siva as co-captains for the 2012-13 season.

Pitino has called him the most complete player on the team and expects him to do a little of everything this year.

"He's not a young kid, he's been through it. With five seconds left in the game if you need to inbound the ball against a press, have him inbound it. If you need somebody to make a shot, have him take the shot. If you need somebody to make the play, have him make the play. If you need a steal or rebound, he'll make it. He's a big time gamer. As of this basketball team, he is much needed," Pitino said.

Like many Cardinals over the past few years, Hancock has struggled with injuries; he separated his shoulder in late April and had surgery on it for precautionary reasons. As the season began, he was still receiving treatment for the injury.

"It's been a little up and down, which I kind of knew it would be. Some days you feel great; some days you don't," Hancock said. "I have learned a lot. My injury kind of held me back this summer, but I feel like I'm getting there. I'm getting ready to go."

Pitino has been adamant about his ability.

"The key to our team though, no question, is Luke

Luke Hancock battles Notre Dame's Pat Connaughton for a rebound during the Cardinals' 73-57 win over the Irish on March 9. The 6-foot-6 junior small forward contributed 10 points and five rebounds to the win. (Austin Lassell/The Louisville Cardinal)

Hancock. We need him on the court. He's an 80 percent foul shooter, a good three-point shooter. He knows how to pass, knows how to play and he will be ready," Pitino said.

"We want to win the Big East," Hancock said, "and make a deep run into the tournament. You know everyone wants to win a national championship. I don't really have personal goals. We just want to win games." ∎

"THE KEY TO OUR TEAM THOUGH, NO QUESTION, IS LUKE HANCOCK. WE NEED HIM ON THE COURT. HE'S AN 80 PERCENT FOUL SHOOTER, A GOOD THREE-POINT SHOOTER. HE KNOWS HOW TO PASS, KNOWS HOW TO PLAY AND HE WILL BE READY."

— Louisville Coach Rick Pitino

Louisville coach Rick Pitino talks to his players, including Luke Hancock (center) during Louisville's March 9 win over Notre Dame. Pitino refers to Hancock as "the key to our team." (Austin Lassell/ The Louisville Cardinal)

Regular Season

Game Date: February 3, 2013 · **Location:** Louisville, Kentucky
Score: Louisville 70, Marquette 51

Louisville Erases Marquette in 'White Out'

Reserves Spark Cardinals to Important Big East Victory

By Sam Draut

The No. 12 University of Louisville men's basketball team defeated the No. 25 Marquette Golden Eagles 70-51 at the KFC Yum! Center on Sunday.

In the annual "White Out" game, junior guard Russ Smith, who finished with 18 points and 5 rebounds, led the 18-4 Cardinals. Senior Peyton Siva added 14 points and 7 assists, the only other Cardinal to score in double figures.

The 15-5 Golden Eagles controlled the pace and took an early 9-1 lead through the first six minutes. But, over the next nine minutes, the Cardinals went on a 24-9 run sparked by reserve forwards Montrezl Harrell and Stephan Van Treese. The two combined for 10 points and nine rebounds.

"I thought our subs gave us a great run there. I think when Montrezl came in...he's a very high percentage shooter, because he dunks 50 percent of his shots, so we got a good run there," head coach Rick Pitino said. "I think certain players don't show up on the stat sheet, but Stephan Van Treese and Montrezl gave us a big lift when we needed it."

After a 1 for 8 start, Louisville finished 27-52 from the field, finishing the game at 51.9 percent, while Marquette went just 19 of 53 from the field.

The Cardinal offense was aided by 15 offensive rebounds. For the game, U of L out-rebounded Marquette 38-26.

"The guards got back and got on the glass. I think we matched their physicality," Siva said. "Coach told us they were going to come in here and be physical with us. I think we did a better job after five minutes of matching their intensity."

Russ Smith elevates toward the basket. Smith led the Cardinals with 18 points as Louisville topped Marquette in the annual "White Out" game. (Jessica Knebel/The Louisville Cardinal)

Center Gorgui Dieng finished with eight points and eight rebounds, and forward Wayne Blackshear contributed with nine points and four rebounds.

Louisville went into halftime up 38-24 and continued to control the game in the second half. The Cardinals stretched their lead to 23 after back-to-back threes from forward Luke Hancock six minutes into the second half.

It was a much-needed performance by the Cardinals, after dropping three straight, U of L has recovered with two consecutive wins, tying them for third place in the Big East at 6-3.

"I thought the whole team did a really good job tonight. I couldn't pick one guy to stand out. I thought they all played good, sound basketball in every phase of the game," Pitino said. ∎

"I THOUGHT THE WHOLE TEAM DID A REALLY GOOD JOB TONIGHT. I COULDN'T PICK ONE GUY TO STAND OUT. I THOUGHT THEY ALL PLAYED GOOD, SOUND BASKETBALL IN EVERY PHASE OF THE GAME."

— Louisville Coach Rick Pitino

Peyton Siva surprises two Marquette defenders with a behind-the-back pass. Siva dished out seven assists in the win. (Jessica Knebel/The Louisville Cardinal)

Cardinal Spirit took flight at the KFC Yum! Center on "White Out" night as a tuxedoed Cardinal Bird (left) led 21,418 spirited fans in support of then-No. 12-ranked Louisville. (Jessica Knebel/The Louisville Cardinal)

2
GUARD

RUSS SMITH

Guard Owns Popular Nickname, Infectious Smile

By Noah Allison • April 2, 2013

"Russdiculous."

Opponents now know why junior guard Russ Smith earned his nickname. He is one of the fastest, niftiest, natural-born scorers in the game of basketball.

In the regular season, he was the second-leading scorer in the Big East. He has led Louisville in scoring in 25 of the 38 games played this season. That trend continued in the NCAA tournament. Smith has led the team in scoring in the first four games; he has scored 104 points and tied a career high, scoring 31 in the Sweet 16 matchup over Oregon.

"Well, to be honest, we have great bigs and great forwards who are able to get the rebound and outlet it quick to me. So when I'm able to get in transition, I think that's when I'm at my best," Smith said.

"But, overall, it's really a team effort," he said. "They're finding me in transition, coming off screens and throwing me on point passes where I can create. So a lot of times it's not the actual scorer, it's the person setting the guy up for it. And I'm getting great outlet passes, great curl passes, great passes fading off screens. I think we're doing a tremendous job just trying to win it, doing whatever you can to win."

Smith's most "Russdiculous" performance was his most recent; in the Elite Eight matchup against Duke when sophomore guard Kevin Ware went down with a broken leg, Smith scored 23 points in spite of the intense emotions from the accident and while losing a key backup that was crucial to the team makeup and style of play. Smith played 34 minutes and had two rebounds and two steals.

Smith is arguably having the best tournament of any player thus far; his performance has thrust him into the national spotlight, but Card Nation has grown accustomed to his heroic play. Throughout the year, Smith has averaged 19 points a game. Of the 718 points he has scored, 215 have come from the free-throw line. His ability to make shots nobody should make and get to the foul line so many times has him always managing to get his due.

"Russ, he's a great basketball player, so anytime we struggle, anytime we grab the ball, he's the first one I'm looking for on the floor. Sometimes, when

Russ Smith shoots a three-pointer against Pittsburgh. The junior guard from Brooklyn was the Big East's second-leading scorer during the regular season. (Austin Lassell/The Louisville Cardinal)

I'm on the floor talking, I'm always saying give him the ball, because once he's got the ball in his hand, he's going to score, get a foul or both," junior center Gorgui Dieng said. "He's doing a great job on this basketball team, and I think we really need him...We just need to give him credit."

And he is not a ball hog; he is an artist with the basketball and points are what he creates. He has scored 223 field goals and has 111 assists. He is second on the team with 81 steals and ferocious with his defensive effort. He is a team player through and through who is capable of taking over if the offense needs to get it going. Versus UConn, Smith had 15 of the 28 first half points, finishing with 23 in a 73-58 victory.

His play is unorthodox, but with Pitino's ability to harness talent, Russ Smith was able to grow from a freshman, who wasn't sure if he was returning for a second season, to a sophomore spark plug of points and energy off the bench to a starting junior, who is a leader and a game changer.

He and senior point guard Peyton Siva make up a potent one-two punch and clearly one of the nation's top backcourts.

Few thought Smith from Brooklyn, N.Y., would be lighting up the stage and leading the Cardinals to consecutive Final Four appearances.

"Because he's not a so-called McDonald's All-American...Russ, actually when I recruited him, lied to me about who was recruiting him. He wasn't recruited by one Big East school, not one," Pitino said. "There are four schools in that area, not one. And basically you look at a player and we got lucky...We have one of the premier players in the country, and he wasn't even recruited." ■

Russ Smith enjoys a lighthearted moment during Louisville's February 23 win over Seton Hall. (Austin Lassell/The Louisville Cardinal)

Russ Smith races downcourt during Louisville's January 28 win over Pittsburgh. More than just a scorer, Smith was second on the team in both steals and assists. (Austin Lassell/The Louisville Cardinal)

Regular Season

Game Date: February 9, 2013 · **Location:** South Bend, Indiana
Score: Notre Dame 104, Louisville 101 5 OT

Irish Top Cards in 5 OT

Teams Battle Through Longest Big East Regular Season Game

By Sam Draut

No. 25 Notre Dame defeated the No. 11 University of Louisville men's basketball team in the fifth overtime in a hotly contested battle in South Bend on Saturday night. The final score was 104-101.

Jerian Grant scored 12 points in the final 45 seconds to help Notre Dame overcome an eight-point deficit in the final minute to force overtime. Grant finished the game with 19 points.

The longest game in Big East regular season history was nothing new for the 19-5 Cardinals, who have gone to overtime with the Fighting Irish six of their eight meetings.

"It's always overtime," said forward Chane Behanan, who led the Cardinals with 30 points and 15 rebounds. "The strongest will survive. They were a great team tonight and made a lot of big shots."

Besides Behanan's career best 30 points, Louisville was led by forward Luke Hancock, who scored 22 points, and guard Russ Smith, who finished with 21 points and 10 rebounds. Center Gorgui Dieng added 17 points and 13 rebounds.

The game that lasted an extra 25 minutes saw 66 fouls and eight players foul out, four from each team.

In the back and forth battle, there was 26 lead changes and 16 ties. In the end, a last-chance shot by Smith that would have tied the game was off target. Notre Dame fans rushed the court in celebration.

Sophomore Chane Behanan, who had 30 points and 15 rebounds while playing 56 minutes during the marathon session of a game, goes at Notre Dame's Zach Auguste. (AP Images)

Louisville guard Peyton Siva, who struggled through one of his worst performances of the season against the Fighting Irish, tries to blow by Notre Dame's freshman big man, Zach Auguste. (AP Images)

COACH

RICK PITINO

Hall-of-Fame-Bound Coach Reaches Seventh Final Four

By Xavier Bleuel • April 9, 2013

Rick Pitino, one of the greatest basketball minds in the history of college basketball, will be inducted into the Naismith Memorial Basketball Hall of Fame in September.

He is appearing in his seventh Final Four and is the only coach in NCAA history to take three different teams to the national semifinals. Pitino won a national title with Kentucky in 1996.

In 2001, Pitino began a new era at University of Louisville men's basketball fresh off a stint in the NBA. He took over a program in desperate need of rejuvenation after Hall of Fame Head Coach Denny Crum retired after 30 years with U of L.

Three years later, in 2004, the Cards made their first trip to the Final Four. They have now returned to the semifinals the last two years. Pitino's up-tempo style and pressure defense has restored the Cardinals to national prominence.

In his first year at Louisville in 2001, he guided an undersized and outmanned squad to a 19-13 record, upsetting the nation's fourth-ranked team along the way to earning a postseason tournament appearance in the NIT.

The following season, the Cardinals reached the No. 2 position in the Associated Press poll after 17 consecutive wins in the beginning of the season, one short of the school record and the second-highest ever in Conference USA history. U of L won its first-ever C-USA Tournament title.

In 28 seasons as a collegiate head coach at five different schools, Pitino has compiled a 662-239 record, winning 73 percent of his games, which ranks him 11th among active coaches. He has a 308-111 record in 12 seasons at U of L. U of L is among the top 15 programs in winning percentage over the last decade under his guidance.

Rick Pitino, 60, was born in New York City and

Rick Pitino, who has taken three different schools to the Final Four, instructs his team during a 64-61 victory against Pitt. (Austin Lassell/The Louisville Cardinal)

was raised in Bayville, N.Y. He was captain of the St. Dominic basketball team in nearby Oyster Bay, Long Island. Pitino holds several scoring records at St. Dominic, where he was captain.

Coach Pitino was a prominent fixture as point guard at UMass, where he graduated in 1974. He ranks eighth all-time in UMass history with 329 career assists and his 168 assists as a senior is the sixth-best single season total of all-time. His claim to fame at UMass was playing with future Hall-of-Famer Julius Erving as a freshman when Dr. J was a senior.

Pitino began his coaching career at the University of Hawaii as a graduate assistant in 1974. He then served two seasons as an assistant at Syracuse under Jim Boeheim from 1976-78.

Pitino was only 25 years old when he accepted his first head coaching job at Boston University in 1978.

Then in 1985, Pitino accepted a job to become the head coach at Providence University, where he guided the Friars to the Final Four in his second season. He rode his momentum off that appearance to coach at the University of Kentucky, where he won the 1996 national championship and made three Final Four appearances.

A 2006 inductee to the New York City Hall of Fame, Pitino has the sixth-highest winning percentage in NCAA Tournament games among active coaches, winning 77.4 percent of his games in the postseason event with a 46-16 record in 18 tournament appearances. He is one of a select group of eight coaches who have taken teams from four different schools to the NCAA tournament.

He is one of five coaches all-time who have reached the Final Four on at least seven occasions. In October 2012, Pitino signed a five-year extension that will keep him as Louisville's head coach through 2022.

Known for displaying his passion on every possession, Rick Pitino barks out orders during Louisville's 72-58 win against St. John's. (Austin Lassell/The Louisville Cardinal)

Pitino and his wife Joanne have five children — Michael, Christopher, Richard, Ryan and Jacqueline — and four grandchildren — Anna, Audrey (Michael's children), Andrew (Christopher) and Ava (Richard).

Louisville's remarkable run to the Final Four in 2011-2012 saved a disappointing regular-season. Entering the Big East tournament as the sixth-seed, not much was expected of the Cardinals. They then donned the infamous infrared jerseys and won the Big East tournament and pulled off four wins in the tournament, falling to the eventual national champions, the University of Kentucky.

Louisville came into 2012-2013 with the same core of players from the Final Four from the year prior. That led to a No. 2 preseason ranking, and the Cards have not disappointed. They won the tournament's No. 1 overall seed.

This season, Pitino picked up his 650th career win against South Florida on Feb. 17, 2013. Louisville, once again, won the Big East Championship and totaled 30-plus wins. This is U of L's 10th final four and Pitino's seventh, ranking him fourth all-time, tied with North Carolina coach Roy Williams. ∎

Two-time NCAA champion coach Rick Pitino takes a knee during his team's 79-61 victory against Seton Hall. (Austin Lassell/The Louisville Cardinal)

Regular Season

Game Date: February 14, 2013 · **Location:** Louisville, Kentucky
Score: Louisville 72, St. John's 58

Louisville Bounces Back

Following 5 OT Loss, Russ Smith Leads Cards Past St. John's

By Randy Whetstone Jr.

Louisville men's basketball players redeemed themselves Thursday night by defeating St. John's after being held captive in a tough five-overtime loss against Notre Dame on Feb. 9.

The Cardinals improved to 20-5 for the season and 8-4 in Big East play. By running the gauntlet in their last outing, the Cardinals came out focused and determined in an all-around performance against the Red Storm.

Louisville was led by terrific backcourt play from Peyton Siva and Russ Smith. The Cards were able to move the ball fluently in the first half. The team ran up and down the floor scoring 13 fast break points. The first half ended with a steal by the Cards and a finish by Blackshear to give Louisville a seven-point lead. Seconds later, Peyton Siva went coast-to-coast for a layup that beat the buzzer before the half.

The team headed to the locker room with a nine-point lead, 32-23.

St. John's started the second half on a 10-0 run, which gave them a one-point lead, 33-32. That seemed to be the only lightning struck by the Red Storm, and the Cards took over from there.

Russ Smith, who led the Cards with 24 points, gave the team momentum with two big three-point shots. Coach Rick Pitino said, "He gave us the spurt we needed."

Louisville maintained the tempo throughout the rest of the heated contest. Gorgui Dieng recorded a double-double with 10 points and 17 rebounds.

Louisville guard Peyton Siva, who had 12 points and six assists against St. John's, deftly goes behind the back for a pass. (Austin Lassell/The Louisville Cardinal)

"WE GOT TO GO DOWN AND JUST KEEP ON GETTING BETTER. OUR GOAL IS TO WIN ALL SEVEN. IT'S A LEAGUE THAT SHOWS NO MERCY."

— Louisville Coach Rick Pitino

The Cardinals will strive to return to the top of the Big East when they face off against South Florida on Feb. 17. Coach Pitino gave his thoughts about the league in the last leg of the regular season.

"We got to go down and just keep on getting better," he said. "Our goal is to win all seven. It's a league that shows no mercy. It's going to be very exciting come Big East tournament time, because it's the last time we all get together.

"All of us are going to miss it very much," Pitino added. "We had something really special, and we let it get away. So, we got to enjoy it one last time around, even though we will play another year, but we won't have Pitt and Syracuse." ■

Burly sophomore Chane Behanan prevents St. John's freshman Chris Obekpa from posting up on the block. (Austin Lassell/The Louisville Cardinal)

5
GUARD

KEVIN WARE

U of L's super sub stays true to his roots

By Noah Allison • February 19, 2013

Louisville's starting backcourt, consisting of senior point guard Peyton Siva and junior shooting guard Russ Smith, is arguably one of the top backcourts in the nation. Their aggressive, fast-paced style of play wears down opponents and leads the Cardinals to victory. Then, in comes No. 5, Kevin Ware.

Ware, the six-foot-two sophomore guard, utilizes his long athletic body to play blanket defense on whomever he needs to. Under the guidance of Coach Rick Pitino and tutelage of Siva and Smith, Ware is developing into a dependable sixth man, who can come in at crucial times throughout the game.

Ware is originally from the Bronx in New York City, and like upperclassman Russ Smith, who is from Brooklyn, he's a product of the historic and cultural basketball upbringing that is associated with everyday life in New York City.

"I've been playing basketball since I can remember being able to walk," Ware said. "I was in New York until I was about 14. Then I moved, and from eighth grade until my senior year I lived in Georgia."

Ware first moved to Atlanta before settling in Rockdale County, a small community on the outskirts of Atlanta.

"My mom is one of those people that likes to just be by herself so it was a bit quiet there," Ware said. "It was difficult because a lot of my family was in New York originally. I had family in Georgia but I was a lot closer to my family in New York, and just moving away from certain people in my family was kind of hard at first. Moving down there and jumping to a whole new kind of city was kind of difficult, but I got used to it."

Ware's early days of growing up playing basketball in New York City can partly correlate to his current position in the game he loves.

"I can say New York City has some of the best guards in the world. You can just go down the list of a million people," Ware said. "I think we are guard-heavy out of New York, where like Indiana you have a variety of big men and shooters, and in Atlanta you have shooting guards and small forwards. But New York is definitely heavy in guards, even the big men can handle the ball like guards and it's always been like that."

Luke Hancock consoles Kevin Ware after the guard suffered the infamous catastrophic leg injury during the Elite Eight game. (Austin Lassell/The Louisville Cardinal)

As Ware continues to develop, he proves to be yet another example of talent that is being polished and harnessed by Coach Pitino and his staff.

"Getting here last year was a great experience. I learned a lot from the second semester of my freshman year and continuing into this season. I didn't really see the difference on the pick and roll until I watched myself last year compared to how I use it this year. Coming off screens, playing defense, there was a lot of stuff that I didn't know that I know now. I can really say that my game has improved a lot, and as long as I'm here it will keep improving," Ware said.

Ware's role on the team is more crucial than his stats may show. His 16 minutes per game help make the Cardinals a top team in the nation. The depth at every position is exemplified by the play of Ware, coming in and being reliable when the team needs him.

"I'm comfortable with my role this year. I feel like as time goes on I'll get more involved at different things but it's not like Coach P. is just all out everything you do is defense; when I get my opportunity, I take it. But we get a lot of scoring from Russ and Peyton already so I just come in and be an energy guy this year," Ware said.

"I love the fast break, when it's me and somebody else one-on-one; I feel like I'm unstoppable, and chasing down blocks I feel like I'm really good at," Ware continued. "And I can go up and get alley-oops. I always tell Peyton just throw it up, and I'll go get it. I tell everybody that, but they feel like if I don't get it then it's a turnover on their part, so they are kind of hesitant a little bit."

For all he can do athletically, Ware is most valuable for his defending. In 24 games he has 21 steals, and what doesn't get recorded are the deflections and forced turnovers he also helps create in the havoc-loving U of L defense.

"I've just always been one of those kind of guys that is not going to let somebody be able to say they were able

During Louisville's title run, sophomore guard Kevin Ware was a key contributor off the bench, adding another presence to one of the best defensive teams in the country. (Austin Lassell/The Louisville Cardinal)

to kill me in any aspect on the court. As long as I can remember, I could successfully guard the best player on the team," Ware said. "When I'm on my guy, I feel like I just have to stop him any way possible. I don't care how I have to do it. I don't want him to have 25 or 30 points on me because that looks bad on me, and I've always been that type of person. But I need to attack more. I feel like offensively I'm a good player, so when I'm on the court I can't just be another guy. I have to make the defense play me."

Ware and the Cardinals only have five regular season games left. Each one will determine the eventual Big East regular season champions. After those five, the real season starts, first with the last true Big East Tournament and then on to the NCAA tournament.

"We need to get back to turning people over. I feel like when we are playing defense and getting after it and getting on the break then that is where we really excel," Ware said. "We struggle sometimes in the half-court setting because sometimes we're on and sometimes we're off. But when we're on a fast break we are set because we have a lot of talented athletes and that's our style of play; when we get after people and turn defense into offense on the break, then we are unstoppable."

Ware's quiet demeanor and sound style of play makes him one of the more mysterious players on the team. While many U of L fans may not know about him, they should all know of him by now. Without the stability that Ware brings to the guard position, Siva and Smith wouldn't be able to play their style of game. If there is any one thing that matters about Ware that the Card Nation should know about him though, it's simply this:

"I'm a good guy, really down to earth," Ware said. "I don't want to come off like a mean person. I know a lot of people think I'm a mean guy, but it's just because I'm so quiet. I really am a nice guy when you talk to me." ■

Part of Louisville's pressing defense, Kevin Ware deflects a ball from Duke point guard Quinn Cook during the Cardinals' 85-63 victory in the Elite Eight game. (Austin Lassell/The Louisville Cardinal)

Big East Tournament Quarterfinals

Game Date: March 14, 2013 · **Location:** New York, New York
Score: Louisville 74, Villanova 55

Louisville Topples Villanova in Big Apple

Smith draws on Strength and Grief to Power Through Win

By Sammie Hill

The Louisville Cardinals opened the Big East Tournament with speed and intensity on Thursday night, earning a 74-55 victory over Villanova. The night held special significance for junior guard Russ Smith. His high school coach, Jack Curran of Archbishop Molloy High School in Queens, New York, had passed away that morning at 82.

"It was really hard for me for about 45 minutes when I was on the bus crying and stuff," Smith said. "It was almost heartbreaking to think about it. I'm going to miss him. He was everything to me, and to my mom, my family. He treated everyone with respect. He taught me a lot of things."

The tragic news devastated Smith, but he used it as inspiration to win the game for his former coach.

"I just wanted to win and do anything I could to win," Smith stated. "Today was definitely Coach Curran Day for me, and it will be the rest of my life."

Smith scored 28 points, leading Louisville to victory. He made 10 of 11 free throws and hit four three-pointers. When diving for a loose ball, Smith twisted his ankle, causing him to limp, but the 6-foot guard would not relent.

"Russ had a heavy heart tonight," said Coach Rick Pitino, who considered Curran a good friend. "I just told Russ we have to play this tournament and the NCAAs for Coach Curran. Coach Curran really enjoyed coaching Russ, and I really enjoy coaching Russ, but we both knew what he was all about. So it's very exciting that Russ could have that type of game and honor his coach like that."

The Cardinals had 58 deflections overall, 38 of which occurred before halftime, setting an all-time high.

"That's never happened in all my years of

Playing in honor of his deceased high school coach, Russ Smith soars to the basket against Villanova during the Big East Tournament. (Getty Images)

"THIS TEAM COULD WIN A NATIONAL CHAMPIONSHIP. YOU TAKE THEIR TALENT AND THEN PUT ON TOP OF THAT THE FACT THAT THEY'VE BEEN THERE THAT EXPERIENCE IS SO VALUABLE."

— Villanova Coach Jay Wright

coaching, so it was an incredible thing to witness. Very, very active," Pitino said. "I think we were just very intense. We were really quick."

After the game, the Cardinals received a visit from an unexpected guest, former President Bill Clinton. Clinton has been a friend of Pitino for years, as the two share a deep love of basketball.

"We got the chance to take a lot of pictures. It was a big treat for our guys," Pitino said. "It was a lot of fun. He was just telling a lot of stories."

Louisville has won its last eight regular-season games. The victory over Villanova marked the Cardinals' sixth consecutive win at Madison Square Garden.

"This team could win a national championship," Villanova head coach Jay Wright said. "You take their talent and then put on top of that the fact that they've been there, that experience is so valuable." ■

Wayne Blackshear, who scored seven points and snared five rebounds against Villanova, lunges for a loose ball. (Getty Images)

Big East Tournament Semifinals

Game Date: March 15, 2013 · **Location:** New York, New York
Score: Louisville 69, Notre Dame 57

Cards Advance to Big East Final – Again

Siva's Double-Double Leads Louisville Past Notre Dame

By Sammie Hill

For the third year in a row, the University of Louisville men's basketball team defeated Notre Dame in the semifinals of the Big East tournament. This year's 69-57 victory holds special meaning, for the Cardinals have earned their place in the championship for the last time before the Big East undergoes massive reconstruction.

"It's very exciting to be in another final game, especially the last year of existence in the Big East," head coach Rick Pitino said. "So we're very excited."

Junior guard Russ Smith also acknowledged the significance of Friday's win.

"It's pretty unbelievable," Smith said. "For this to be the last tournament of the Big East as it really is, as the power basketball conference that it is, it's pretty special."

Smith scored 20 points against Notre Dame, while senior guard Peyton Siva earned 12 points and six assists.

"Peyton Siva kept bailing us out one rotation after another," Pitino said. "He's just an incredible player."

Siva also had seven steals, propelling him past the legendary Darrell Griffith as Louisville's career steals leader.

"When you realize the talent we've had at Louisville," Pitino explained, "one of the greatest traditions in all of college basketball, Siva's accomplishment is saying something because they've had so many great athletes, so many great players."

Pitino went on to praise not only the caliber of Siva's play but also the quality of his character.

"I keep repeating it over and over and over," he said. "The two greatest people I've ever coached in my life were Billy Donovan and Siva—just as people. And then you match the

Coach Rick Pitino instructs Gorgui Dieng, who collected 12 rebounds and four blocks in the 69-57 victory against Notre Dame. (Getty Images)

98

"THE TWO GREATEST PEOPLE I'VE EVER COACHED IN MY LIFE WERE BILLY DONOVAN AND SIVA."

— Louisville Coach Rick Pitino

fact that they were both great point guards. So I've been very, very lucky to have coached Billy, and now I'm very lucky to coach Peyton."

Siva had a different explanation for his standout play.

"People keep telling me not to back up and keep running aggressively, and that's what I try to do," Siva said. "The ball just came to me tonight. It's as easy as that."

In Louisville's fourth Big East championship appearance in five years, the Cardinals will take on Syracuse, who they defeated in 2009 to win the title.

"I hope we own it tomorrow," Siva said of the championship game. "I think around this time of year Coach really pushes us to bring our game to a higher level."

Syracuse and Louisville have met twice this season with each team winning at home. Syracuse won 70-68 on Jan. 19, while Louisville won 58-53 on March 2. The Cardinals will strive to defeat the Orange on Saturday in hopes of capturing their second consecutive Big East tournament title. ■

Coach Rick Pitino (far left) and the Cardinal bench react during Louisville's 69-57 victory over Notre Dame. (Getty Images)

Big East Tournament Title Game
Game Date: March 16, 2013 · **Location:** New York, New York
Score: Louisville 78, Syracuse 61

U of L's wins second consecutive Big East Tournament

Cards come from behind to soundly defeat Syracuse
By Xavier Bleuel

A whirlwind of emotions came swooping in a few moments after the buzzer sounded on Saturday night. The Louisville Cardinals won the Big East Championship, 78-61 over Syracuse, but something more meaningful was upon us.

This was finally it. The Big East as we know it was no more. It's not like the end came as a surprise. We all knew it was coming, but we're never fully prepared to see the conference that Dave Gavitt built from the ground up in the late 1970s disband.

Louisville Coach Rick Pitino, showcasing his utmost respect for the conference that made him into who he is today, told his team to not cut the nets down in Madison Square Garden.

"Obviously, it's a real special night for the University of Louisville," Pitino said. "The final minute of play, first thing I thought of is what an incredible group of guys I'm coaching. Then I thought how happy I was for my family, and then immediately I thought of (Big East founder and first commissioner) Dave Gavitt and what

he formed, and all of us in some way or another flourish because of Dave Gavitt."

After a dominating first half and first four minutes of the second, the Orange were up 45-29 with 15 minutes to play, it seemed like a perfect ending for Syracuse (26-9, 11-7) and the Big East, one of its long-standing members to win the final game of the conference.

However, the Cardinals (29-5, 14-4) had other plans.

Led by freshman forward Montrezl Harrell, the Cards overcame the largest deficit in the Big East Championship history to cruise past Syracuse 78-61. Harrell scored a career-high 20 points, while adding seven rebounds, igniting the comeback.

"I came in the game just being prepared for

The Cardinals celebrate their Big East Tournament championship, which helped Louisville sew up the No. 1 overall seed in the NCAA Tournament. (Michelle Hutchins/Louisville Athletics)

102

whatever coach needed me to do," Harrell said. "When I got on the floor, I just wanted to help guys with a big lift. I was going all over the place, trying to get rebounds, either offense or defense. These guys looked for me, and I just tried to finish for them. I just came out hard and played my heart out."

To say it was remarkable would be an understatement. The Cards pressed, then pressed, then pressed some more. The Cardinals blitzed and confused the Orange in the second half, forcing 13 turnovers and scoring 25 points off those mistakes.

"I think they're the best pressing team that I've seen this year," Syracuse Coach Jim Boeheim said. "It was probably the worst thing to happen to get up 15. If we hadn't played well and we were up four or five, they probably wouldn't have done that, but that's what they had to do at that point to go after it, and that was exactly what I would have tried to do, and that's what they did, and they're good at it."

Being down by 16 can rattle some teams and psychologically send them packing. The Cardinals, however, aren't your average team. Senior guard Peyton Siva would not let a loss be his lasting memory in the Big East wearing the jersey that he worked so hard to earn.

"I knew we would come back," Siva, who became the school's all-time steals leader, said during the on-court celebration. "It might not be the prettiest win in the beginning, but we got the job done."

Despite just joining the conference in 2005, the Cardinals can be proud of their accomplishments during their short time in the conference.

The Cardinals double-dipped as regular season and conference champions during the Big East's final season; they won their second straight championship in the perennially strongest basketball conference in America.

As the icing on the cake, the Cardinals hold the honor of being the last champions of the Big East in football and basketball. ▪

Freshman forward Montrezl Harrell throws down a dunk during Louisville's 78-61 victory against Syracuse in the Big East Tournament. (Michelle Hutchins/Louisville Athletics)

NCAA Tournament Second Round

Game Date: March 21, 2013 · **Location:** Lexington, Kentucky
Score: Louisville 79, North Carolina A&T 48

Louisville Destroys No. 16 Seed

Smith, Cards Force 27 Turnovers in Rout

By Noah Allison

Early in the season, Louisville head coach Rick Pitino said that this could be the year that a No. 16 seed beats a No. 1 seed in the NCAA tournament. Heading into this year's tournament, his Cardinals were the No. 1 overall seed, playing a 16 seed North Carolina A&T team that won its first ever tournament game when they defeated Liberty 73-72 in the Midwest play-in game.

If the Big Dance were an actual dance off, the North Carolina A&T Bulldog mascot could have made it a long night for Louisville fans.

Unfortunately for A&T, the game was decided on the court, and the Cardinals stole the show. In the Cardinals' 79-48 victory, the team set an NCAA tournament single-game record with 20 steals. Russ Smith led the team in steals with eight and in scoring with 23 points.

Four minutes into the first half, North Carolina A&T kept it close, only down 6-4. Then Pitino let the dogs loose, and A&T struggled making it past the half-court line. The Cardinals

forced them into 27 turnovers, had 67 deflections and caused a 10-second half court violation and 35-second shot clock violation.

"We approached it as we can't take any team lightly. They are in the NCAA tournament so they did something right to get here. We have to take it one game at a time," sophomore guard Kevin Ware said.

"We go so hard in the summertime with conditioning and lifting that it gives us the upper hand on a lot of the teams we play. It really starts with defense, and that's all we go over in the summertime, and around this time of year

The suffocating defense of Stephan Van Treese (44) and Russ Smith (2) helped force 27 turnovers during Louisville's resounding victory against North Carolina A&T. (Austin Lassell/The Louisville Cardinal)

"IT REALLY STARTS WITH DEFENSE, AND THAT'S ALL WE GO OVER IN THE SUMMERTIME, AND AROUND THIS TIME OF YEAR TEAMS GET A LITTLE FATIGUED WITH ONE GAME PREPARATION AND NOT A LOT OF TIME TO REST AND THAT HELPS US."

— Louisville Guard Kevin Ware

teams get a little fatigued with one game preparation and not a lot of time to rest and that helps us."

While the Cardinals lightning fast guards on the full court harassed the Aggies, they were also dominated by Louisville's size in the paint. Louisville had 31 rebounds to A&T's 20 and had 44 points in the paint compared with A&T's 16.

The Aggies did what they could to hang around and multiple times when it looked like the Cards were going to put the dagger in early A&T fought back, but the constant nuisance of Louisville's defense wore their shallow rotation down. A&T did not get the contribution from the bench that is necessary when playing a team as conditioned as Louisville. U of L's bench outscored A&T's 22 points to eight. ∎

Louisville guard Russ Smith tries to swipe the ball away from North Carolina A&T guard Jean Louisme. (Austin Lassell/The Louisville Cardinal)

NCAA Tournament Third Round

Game Date: March 23, 2013 · **Location:** Lexington, Kentucky
Score: Louisville 82, Colorado State 56

Cards Own 'Russ Arena'

U of L Defense Runs Veteran Rams Team Ragged

By Noah Allison

In their second game of the tournament in the home of the Kentucky Wildcats, the Cards faced the top rebounding team in the country, and earned a victory that will launch them into the next round of the NCAA tournament, the Sweet 16. Colorado State started five seniors and took the court as one of the most veteran and competitive teams the Cards have faced all year. Colorado State rolled through Missouri winning 84-72 in their first game and came into the game against Louisville hot.

The Rams sank their first six shots from the floor and matched U of L point for point through the beginning minutes of the game. The game was tied at 18 when U of L's defense took over. By halftime the score was 45-31 in Louisville's favor, and by the end, Louisville had long ensured its 82-56 victory.

As badly as Colorado State wanted to control the pace of this game, U of L imposed its will on the Rams, forcing 20 turnovers, winning the rebound battle and outscoring Colorado State in the paint 42 to 14. Junior guard Russ Smith went 4-6 from behind the three-point line in the first half and ended the game with 27 points.

"They were shooting at a high percentage, but we were turning them over," senior guard Peyton Siva said. "Russ caught fire again. He loves playing here, so we just tried feeding him the ball and for the most part we did a great job at out rebounding them. We out-rebounded them tonight, and that was our main focus."

It isn't easy to rattle a team that has five starting seniors who can handle the ball, shoot at a high percentage and rebound at a high rate,

Russ Smith looks to pass against Colorado State. Smith scored 27 points, including four three-pointers, as the Cardinals advanced to the Sweet 16. (Austin Lassell/The Louisville Cardinal)

> ## "COACH SAID BEFORE THE GAME, THEY ONLY AVERAGE 10 TURNOVERS A GAME, BUT THAT DOES NOT MEAN WE CAN'T TURN THEM OVER....I THINK THE WHOLE TEAM PLAYED A GOOD GAME TONIGHT."

— Louisville Center Gorgui Dieng

but if there is one way to describe the Colorado State players halfway through their experience with the No. 1 ranked team in the country, it was rattled.

"Coach said before the game, they only average 10 turnovers a game, but that does not mean we can't turn them over. I think they started to feel fatigued and that's why they started missing free throws and turning the ball over. I think the whole team played a good game tonight," junior center Gorgui Dieng said. "At this time of the year, we don't need somebody to just have a great game; we need the whole team to step up. I think everybody did their job tonight and that's the way we need to play."

The Cardinals won both of their games at Rupp Arena by more than 25 points. Smith had a combined 50 points in his two games there, making his case for changing the name to "Russ Arena." ∎

Forward Montrezl Harrell lays the ball up against Colorado State. The freshman came off the bench to score 11 points in 20 minutes. (Austin Lassell/The Louisville Cardinal)

NCAA Tournament Sweet 16

Game Date: March 29, 2013 · **Location:** Indianapolis, Indiana
Score: Louisville 77, Oregon 69

Cardinals Overcome Illness, Ducks

Smith Scores 31 Points for Cardinals' 13th-Straight Win

By Noah Allison

With a cold plaguing the Louisville Cardinals, the best remedy did not seem to be a serving of hot duck. The Pac-12 tournament champion Oregon Ducks faired better against the Cardinals than Louisville's first two round competitors, but they could not keep junior guard Russ Smith from tying his career high by scoring 31 points in the Cardinals' 77-69 Sweet 16 victory.

"Unfortunately, Russ has infected our entire team with a ridiculous cold, and all our guys are really sick," head coach Rick Pitino said. "It took a lot out of us because Oregon's so good. When Peyton got in foul trouble, Russ had to play way too many minutes, and everybody's coughing and hacking at every timeout. We just had to get our guys through it, and hopefully we'll get better."

Pitino remains undefeated in the Sweet 16 and is now 11-0 when he has a week to prepare for the opponent he faces in the Sweet 16.

"He's just a great coach. He prepares us so well before each game that we know everything the other team is going to do. We know every detail. If we have time to prepare, it's really tough for the opponent because we go over every play and everything we need to know to win," senior center Stephan Van Treese said.

Smith had a career game in his takeover of this NCAA tournament, but the team also got considerable contributions from the big man junior center Gorgui Dieng, who came in and grabbed nine rebounds, had four blocked shots and scored 10 points. Sophomore guard Kevin Ware had a steal and a career high 11 points as his role becomes more and more crucial to the team's success.

"Kevin plays so hard and he just wants to do good, contribute and he was very focused before

Oregon forward E.J. Singler tries to defend Russ Smith, who had a game-high 31 during the Sweet 16 contest. (Tricia Stern/The Louisville Cardinal)

"UNFORTUNATELY, RUSS HAS INFECTED OUR ENTIRE TEAM WITH A RIDICULOUS COLD, AND ALL OUR GUYS ARE REALLY SICK."

— Louisville Coach Rick Pitino

the game. I spoke with him, and he was just telling me how well he's going to do," Smith said. "He was so confident today, and I'm so happy for him. His lift was just big, and for Peyton to go out from foul trouble and being sick and Kevin Ware to step up like that. That just goes to show you how deep we are."

"I just feel like I'm playing my best basketball right now," Ware said. "I have to take my advantages when they open the lane and I have to use my athleticism to get to the basket and I have to be aggressive and attack.

"At this point coach is telling me that I need to make mistakes. 'Just don't go out there and sit around and not do anything,'" Ware added. "He's been telling me that for a while now honestly. Peyton (Siva) is my roommate back home, and he always tells me those tips of what to do and what not to do on screens or playing defense. He's always been there for me, him and Russ."

In the Cardinals' 13 game win streak, Ware has proved to be invaluable to the team's style of play and success. When he comes off the bench, there is no letup in the guard play.

"I feel like I've had a lot of growth since my suspension in March for the Pittsburgh game," Ware said. "I feel like that was a wake-up call for me honestly. I can't waste this scholarship. I need to go out there, contribute and do what I need to do." ∎

Though limited by foul trouble through much of the game, Louisville guard Peyton Siva drives on backup guard Johnathan Loyd. (Tricia Stern/The Louisville Cardinal)

Strong fan support at the opulent, 22,000-seat KFC Yum! Center helped push the Cardinals toward a championship season. (Austin Lassell/The Louisville Cardinal)

NCAA Tournament Elite Eight
Game Date: March 31, 2013 · **Location:** Indianapolis, Indiana
Score: Louisville 85, Duke 63

Taking Kevin Ware to His Atlanta Home

Defensive Stand, Heavy Emotion Propel Cards to Final Four

By Noah Allison and Xavier Bleuel

On Sunday in Indianapolis, after an 85-63 defeat of the Duke Blue Devils in the Elite Eight, the Cardinals held up two trophies. One, a Midwest Regional trophy for going to the program's second straight Final Four, the other, Kevin Ware's No. 5 jersey.

For everyone around the nation who was watching, this was no mere basketball game. The first 13 minutes were as competitive as anyone could have expected out of this matchup of historic programs and legendary coaches. The game was played with the intensity of a national championship, but that game ended with the Cardinals leading 21-20.

With 6:33 remaining in the first half, Duke player Tyler Thornton made a three-point shot attempt that was contested by Louisville's emerging sophomore Kevin Ware. Ware had a career high 11 points in the previous Sweet 16 win against Oregon. Ware jumped, landed and fell to the ground directly in front of the Cardinal bench with his right leg visibly broken. The crowd was shocked and even the commentators were speechless. Cardinal players were sobbing

and Rick Pitino was wiping away his own tears while trying to remain strong. Everyone seemed to be focused on Ware's injury, except Ware.

"I don't think any of us, with what we had to witness, could have overcome it," Coach Pitino said, "if it wasn't for Kevin Ware, 12 times saying to the guys, 'I'll be fine. Win the game!'"

From 6:33 on, a new game was played, a game to get Ware back home to Atlanta. For the first time all year, the No. 1 team in the country had an inspired reason to play.

Junior guard Russ Smith continued his takeover of the tournament and led the Cardinals with 23 points. Junior center Gorgui Dieng made his presence felt with 14 points, 11 rebounds and four blocked shots. Sophomore forward Chane Behanan brought in eight rebounds, eight points and led the team in steals

Forward Chane Behanan raises the jersey of his close friend and fellow sophomore Kevin Ware, who endured a horrific injury during the Elite Eight contest. (Austin Lassell/The Louisville Cardinal)

The Cardinals, who drew inspiration from their fallen comrade, hold the jersey of Kevin Ware during their postgame celebration. (Austin Lassell/The Louisville Cardinal)

with three. Senior guard Peyton Siva dished out four assists to go along with his 16 points.

"First, when Kevin went down, it was devastating for all of us," Siva said. "But we just came together, and Kevin Ware really was the reason why we pulled this game out. I don't know how he got the strength to do it, but he told us to go out there and win."

Louisville's defense shut Duke down with nine blocked shots. Duke turned the ball over 12 times. Duke's Seth Curry, who had 29 points and six 3-pointers in the Sweet 16 win over Michigan State, was scoreless in the first half and held to 12 points overall. When the game was tied at 42, U of L went on a defensive stand that left Duke without a field goal for eight minutes. The best defensive team in the country outscored Duke 50-31 in the second half.

"I just said to them over and over and over, and at halftime, 'We know our game plan offensively and defensively. If we let up for a second, then Kevin Ware doesn't mean how much he means to us. We're going to dig in. We're going to play this game to the end. We'll get him back home, nurse him to good health, and we're going to get him to Atlanta,'" Pitino said.

The aftermath of Ware's gruesome injury was something no one present would ever forget. "I heard it pop," Smith said. "I never thought in a million years that I would see something like that, especially to someone like Kevin Ware."

Senior guard Siva and junior guard Smith dropped to the ground while sophomore forward Behanan, who is a close friend of Ware, fell to the court in agonizing disbelief.

"The bond Chane and Kevin share is unmatched in the locker room," Smith stated. "They're on a whole different level; they're brothers."

The players on the bench reacted immediately as they saw their teammate's disfigured leg while Pitino wiped away tears.

"That was the worst thing I have witnessed on the basketball court," said Pitino. "I've been through worse during 9/11 and losing a son, but nothing ever like that in front of my players."

Louisville point guard Peyton Siva, who scored 16 points and dished out four assists in the victory against Duke, helped control the Elite Eight game. (Austin Lassell/The Louisville Cardinal)

"THIS YEAR WAS ABOUT HUMILITY. THE ONE THING THAT COULD BEAT US WAS LACK OF HUMILITY. THE GUYS WERE GREAT AT THAT. THEY ALL BOUGHT IN. THEY KNOW WHAT IT IS TO PLAY FOR LOUISVILLE."

— Louisville Coach Rick Pitino

While being attended to on the court, Ware tried to get the attention of his teammates but they couldn't hear them.

"Guys!" Pitino yelled. "He wants to say something."

The team surrounded Ware and he told them what is now the team's new rallying cry, "Just win it for me, y'all."

During halftime, Pitino gathered his somber bunch and told his team to win for Ware. Tears were abundant while the Cardinals tried to regroup. Ware is an Atlanta native, who played high school ball 24 miles from the Georgia Dome, the site of the Final Four.

"We couldn't lose this game for him," Pitino stated. "We just couldn't."

The Cardinals have won 14 games in a row, and they are going back to the Final Four for the second consecutive year. Smith is dominating the tournament with 101 points, scoring at least 20 in all four games thus far.

"We knew all along that we were good, and we knew how great of a team we are," Smith said. "Coach knew it, the whole staff knew it. We had faith in each other. All we had to do was put it together."

This will be U of L's 10th trip to the Final Four, and they head down to Atlanta with a mission.

"This year was about humility," Pitino explained. "The one thing that could beat us was a lack of humility. The guys were great at that. They all bought in. They know what it is to play for Louisville."

"It's going to be a heck of a Final Four," Pitino continued. "I'm just really, really pleased that it's Kevin's home and we can get him back home." ◾

Part of a defensive effort that frustrated Duke all game long, Russ Smith (2) and Wayne Blackshear (20) trap Duke guard Tyler Thornton. (Austin Lassell/The Louisville Cardinal)

Celebrating his second consecutive Final Four appearance, Russ Smith jumps into the arms of Andre McGee, Louisville's director of operations. (Austin Lassell/The Louisville Cardinal)